POETRY

ANTHOLOGY

FOR

OCR AS ENGLISH
LITERATURE

OCR
RECOGNISING ACHIEVEMENT

OXFORD
UNIVERSITY PRESS

Official Publisher Partnership

OXFORD
UNIVERSITY PRESS

Oxford University Press is a department of the University of Oxford. It furthers the University's objective of
excellence in research, scholarship, and education by publishing worldwide in

Oxford New York

Auckland Cape Town Dar es Salaam Hong Kong Karachi
Kuala Lumpur Madrid Melbourne Mexico City Nairobi
New Delhi Shanghai Taipei Toronto

With offices in

Argentina Austria Brazil Chile Czech Republic France Greece Guatemala Hungary
Italy Japan South Korea Poland Portugal Singapore Switzerland Thailand Turkey Ukraine Vietnam

British Library Cataloguing in Publication Data

Data available

ISBN: 978-0-19-838695-7

10 9 8 7 6 5 4 3

Printed by Bell and Bain Ltd,. Glasgow.

Paper used in the production of this book is a natural, recyclable product made from wood grown
in sustainable forests. The manufacturing process conforms to the environmental regulations
of the country of origin.

Acknowledgements

Robert Frost: all poems from *The Poetry of Robert Frost* edited by Edward Connery Lathem (Jonathan Cape, 1971),
reprinted by permission of The Random House Group on behalf of the Estate of Robert Frost.

Wilfred Owen: all poems from *Collected Poems of Wilfred Owen*, W.W. Norton & Co Ltd; Revised Ed edition (1 Feb
1965).

Christina Rossetti: all poems from *Christina Rossetti: The Complete Poems* edited by R.W. Crump, Penguin Classics;
New Ed edition (26 Jul 2001).

William Wordsworth: all poems from *William Wordsworth: The Major Works*, edited by Stephen Gill, Oxford World's
Classics; New Ed edition (27 Jul 2000).

Mixed Sources
Product group from well-managed
forests and other controlled sources
www.fsc.org Cert no. TT-COC-002769
© 1996 Forest Stewardship Council
FSC

Contents

Contents

OCR Specification Excerpt

The OCR GCE specification for English Literature is the document on which assessment is based; it specifies the content and skills to be covered in delivering a course of study. At all times, therefore, these excerpts should be read in conjunction with the specification. If clarification on a particular point is needed then reference should be in the first instance to the specification.

Unit Content

AS Unit F661: *Poetry and Prose 1800–1945* (Closed text)

- Section A: Poetry 1800–1945
- Section B: Prose 1800–1945

Section A: Poetry 1800–1945

The focus of this section is the study of selected poems of one poet. Candidates answer one question on one poem of the poet studied.
Candidates should be able to:
- analyse the effects of language, imagery and verse form structure;
- demonstrate understanding of the significance of the contexts in which the poem was written and received, by making appropriate reference to other poems of the same poet.

AS GCE Scheme of Assessment

AS Unit F661: *Poetry and Prose 1800–1945*

60% of the total AS GCE marks
2 h written paper 60 marks

Section A: Poetry

Candidates answer **one** question on **one** poem.
Candidates are assessed on:
AO1: articulate, creative, informed and relevant responses to literary texts, using appropriate terminology and concepts, and coherent, accurate written expression;
AO2: demonstrate detailed critical understanding in analysing the ways in which structure, form and language shape meanings in literary texts;
AO4: demonstrate understanding of the significance and influence of the contexts in which literary texts are written and received.

Assessment Criteria for AS Unit F661: Poetry and Prose 1800–1945

Band	AO	Criteria
Band 6 **26–30** **marks**	AO 1	• excellent and consistently detailed understanding of poem and question; • consistently fluent and accurate writing in appropriate register; • critical terminology used accurately and consistently; • well-structured, coherent and detailed argument consistently developed.
	AO 2	• well-developed and consistently detailed discussion of effects of language, imagery and verse form; • excellent and consistently effective use of analytical methods; • consistently effective use of quotations and references to text, critically addressed, blended into discussion.
	AO 4	• consistently developed and consistently detailed understanding of the significance and influence of contexts in which literary texts are written and understood, as appropriate to the question.
Band 5 **21–25** **marks**	AO 1	• good and secure understanding of poem and question; • good level of coherence and accuracy in writing, in appropriate register; • critical terminology used accurately; • well-structured argument, with clear line of development.
	AO 2	• developed and good level of detail in discussion of effects of language, imagery and verse form; • good use of analytical methods; • good use of quotations and references to text, generally critically addressed.
	AO 4	• good, clear evaluation of the significance and influence of contexts in which literary texts are written and understood, as appropriate to the question.
Band 4 **16–20** **marks**	AO 1	• competent understanding of poem and question; • clear writing in generally appropriate register; • critical terminology appropriately deployed; • straightforward arguments competently structured.
	AO 2	• generally developed discussion of effects of language, imagery and verse form; • competent use of analytical methods; • competent use of illustrative quotations and references to support discussion.
	AO 4	• competent understanding of the significance and influence of contexts in which literary texts are written and understood, as appropriate to the question.
Band 3 **11–15** **marks**	AO 1	• some understanding of poem and main elements of question; • some clear writing, some inconsistencies in register; • some appropriate use of critical terminology; • some structured argument evident, lacking development and/or full illustration.
	AO 2	• some attempt to develop discussion of effects of language, imagery and verse form; • some attempt at using analytical methods; • some use of quotations/references as illustration.
	AO 4	• some understanding of the significance and influence of contexts in which literary texts are written and understood, as appropriate to the question.
Band 2 **6–10** **marks**	AO 1	• limited understanding of poem and partial attempt at question; • inconsistent writing, frequent instances of technical error, limited use of appropriate register; • limited use of critical terminology; • limited attempt to structure discussion; tendency to lose track of argument.
	AO 2	• limited discussion of effects of language, imagery and verse form; • descriptive or narrative comment; limited use of analytical methods; • limited or inconsistent use of quotations, uncritically presented.
	AO 4	• limited understanding of the significance and influence of contexts in which literary texts are written and understood, as appropriate to the question.
Band 1 **0–5** **marks**	AO 1	• very little or no connection with poem, question disregarded; • persistent serious writing errors inhibit communication of meaning, very little or no use of appropriate register; • persistently inaccurate, or no use of critical terminology; • undeveloped, very fragmentary discussion.
	AO 2	• very little or no relevant discussion of effects of language, imagery and verse form; • only very infrequent phrases of commentary; very little or no use of analytical methods; • very few quotations (e.g. one or two) used (and likely to be incorrect), or no quotations used.
	AO 4	• very little reference (and likely to be irrelevant) or no understanding of the significance and influence of contexts in which literary texts are written and understood, as appropriate to the question.

SECTION

ONE

WILLIAM **WORDSWORTH**

Old Man Travelling

Animal Tranquillity and Decay, a Sketch

The little hedge-row birds,	1
That peck along the road, regard him not.	
He travels on, and in his face, his step,	
His gait, is one expression; every limb,	
His look and bending figure, all bespeak	
A man who does not move with pain, but moves	
With thought—He is insensibly subdued	
To settled quiet: he is one by whom	
All effort seems forgotten, one to whom	
Long patience has such mild composure given,	10
That patience now doth seem a thing, of which	
He hath no need. He is by nature led	
To peace so perfect, that the young behold	
With envy, what the old man hardly feels.	
—I asked him whither he was bound, and what	
The object of his journey; he replied	
'Sir! I am going many miles to take	
A last leave of my son, a mariner,	
Who from a sea-fight has been brought to Falmouth,	
And there is dying in an hospital.—'	20

[1798]

Animal Tranquillity and Decay

The little hedgerow birds,   1
That peck along the road, regard him not.
He travels on, and in his face, his step,
His gait, is one expression: every limb,
His look and bending figure, all bespeak
A man who does not move with pain, but moves
With thought.—He is insensibly subdued
To settled quiet: he is one by whom
All effort seems forgotten; one to whom
Long patience hath such mild composure given,   10
That patience now doth seem a thing of which
He hath no need. He is by nature led
To peace so perfect that the young behold
With envy, what the Old Man hardly feels.

[1815]

'Old Man Travelling' represents the poem as published in the first volume of
Lyrical Ballads (1798); the later, shorter version of the poem is how William
Wordsworth determined it should appear in later collections of his work.

Simon Lee, the Old Huntsman

With an incident in which he was concerned

In the sweet shire of Cardigan,   1
Not far from pleasant Ivor-hall,
An old man dwells, a little man,
I've heard he once was tall.
Of years he has upon his back,
No doubt, a burthen weighty;
He says he is three score and ten,
But others say he's eighty.

A long blue livery-coat has he,
That's fair behind, and fair before;   10
Yet, meet him where you will, you see
At once that he is poor.
Full five and twenty years he lived
A running huntsman merry;
And, though he has but one eye left,
His cheek is like a cherry.

No man like him the horn could sound,
And no man was so full of glee;
To say the least, four counties round
Had heard of Simon Lee;   20
His master's dead, and no one now
Dwells in the hall of Ivor;
Men, dogs, and horses, all are dead;
He is the sole survivor.

His hunting feats have him bereft
Of his right eye, as you may see:
And then, what limbs those feats have left
To poor old Simon Lee!
He has no son, he has no child,
His wife, an aged woman,   30
Lives with him, near the waterfall,
Upon the village common.

And he is lean and he is sick,
His little body's half awry;
His ancles they are swoln and thick;
His legs are thin and dry.
When he was young he little knew
Of husbandry or tillage;
And now he's forced to work, though weak,
—The weakest in the village.   40

He all the country could outrun,
Could leave both man and horse behind;
And often, ere the race was done,
He reeled and was stone-blind.
And still there's something in the world
At which his heart rejoices;
For when the chiming hounds are out,
He dearly loves their voices!

Old Ruth works out of doors with him,
And does what Simon cannot do;   50
For she, not over stout of limb,
Is stouter of the two.
And though you with your utmost skill
From labour could not wean them,
Alas! 'tis very little, all
Which they can do between them.

Beside their moss-grown hut of clay,
Not twenty paces from the door,
A scrap of land they have, but they
Are poorest of the poor.   60
This scrap of land he from the heath
Enclosed when he was stronger;
But what avails the land to them,
Which they can till no longer?

Few months of life has he in store,
As he to you will tell,
For still, the more he works, the more
His poor old ancles swell.
My gentle reader, I perceive
How patiently you've waited,   70
And I'm afraid that you expect
Some tale will be related.

O reader! had you in your mind
Such stores as silent thought can bring,
O gentle reader! you would find
A tale in every thing.
What more I have to say is short,
I hope you'll kindly take it;
It is no tale; but should you think,
Perhaps a tale you'll make it.   80

One summer-day I chanced to see
This old man doing all he could
About the root of an old tree,
A stump of rotten wood.
The mattock tottered in his hand;
So vain was his endeavour
That at the root of the old tree
He might have worked for ever.

'You're overtasked, good Simon Lee,
Give me your tool' to him I said;   90
And at the word right gladly he
Received my proffered aid.
I struck, and with a single blow
The tangled root I severed,
At which the poor old man so long
And vainly had endeavoured.

The tears into his eyes were brought,
And thanks and praises seemed to run
So fast out of his heart, I thought
They never would have done.   100
—I've heard of hearts unkind, kind deeds
With coldness still returning.
Alas! the gratitude of men
Has oftner left me mourning.

Anecdote for Fathers

Shewing how the art of lying may be taught

I have a boy of five years old,   1
His face is fair and fresh to see;
His limbs are cast in beauty's mould,
And dearly he loves me.

One morn we strolled on our dry walk,
Our quiet house all full in view,
And held such intermitted talk
As we are wont to do.

My thoughts on former pleasures ran;
I thought of Kilve's delightful shore,   10
My pleasant home, when spring began,
A long, long year before.

A day it was when I could bear
To think, and think, and think again;
With so much happiness to spare,
I could not feel a pain.

My boy was by my side, so slim
And graceful in his rustic dress!
And oftentimes I talked to him,
In very idleness.   20

The young lambs ran a pretty race;
The morning sun shone bright and warm;
'Kilve,' said I, 'was a pleasant place,
And so is Liswyn farm.

'My little boy, which like you more,'
I said and took him by the arm—
'Our home by Kilve's delightful shore,
Or here at Liswyn farm?'

'And tell me, had you rather be,'
I said and held him by the arm,   30
'At Kilve's smooth shore by the green sea,
Or here at Liswyn farm?'

In careless mood he looked at me,
While still I held him by the arm,
And said, 'At Kilve I'd rather be
Than here at Liswyn farm.'

'Now, little Edward, say why so;
My little Edward, tell me why;'
'I cannot tell, I do not know.'
'Why this is strange,' said I.   40

'For, here are woods, and green-hills warm;
There surely must some reason be
Why you would change sweet Liswyn farm
For Kilve by the green sea.'

At this, my boy, so fair and slim,
Hung down his head, nor made reply;
And five times did I say to him,
'Why? Edward, tell me why?'

His head he raised—there was in sight,
It caught his eye, he saw it plain—   50
Upon the house-top, glittering bright,
A broad and gilded vane.

Then did the boy his tongue unlock,
And thus to me he made reply;
'At Kilve there was no weather-cock,
And that's the reason why.'

O dearest, dearest boy! my heart
For better lore would seldom yearn,
Could I but teach the hundredth part
Of what from thee I learn.   60

Expostulation and Reply

'Why William, on that old grey stone,   1
Thus for the length of half a day,
Why William, sit you thus alone,
And dream your time away?

Where are your books? that light bequeathed
To beings else forlorn and blind!
Up! Up! and drink the spirit breathed
From dead men to their kind.

You look round on your mother earth,
As if she for no purpose bore you;   10
As if you were her first-born birth,
And none had lived before you!'

One morning thus, by Esthwaite lake,
When life was sweet I knew not why,
To me my good friend Matthew spake,
And thus I made reply.

'The eye it cannot chuse but see,
We cannot bid the ear be still;
Our bodies feel, where'er they be,
Against, or with our will.   20

Nor less I deem that there are powers,
Which of themselves our minds impress,
That we can feed this mind of ours,
In a wise passiveness.

Think you, 'mid all this mighty sum
Of things for ever speaking,
That nothing of itself will come,
But we must still be seeking?

—Then ask not wherefore, here, alone,
Conversing as I may,   30
I sit upon this old grey stone,
And dream my time away.'

The Tables Turned

An evening scene, on the same subject

Up! up! my friend, and clear your looks,   1
Why all this toil and trouble?
Up! up! my friend, and quit your books,
Or surely you'll grow double.

The sun above the mountain's head,
A freshening lustre mellow,
Through all the long green fields has spread,
His first sweet evening yellow.

Books! 'tis a dull and endless strife,
Come, hear the woodland linnet,   10
How sweet his music; on my life
There's more of wisdom in it.

And hark! how blithe the throstle sings!
And he is no mean preacher;
Come forth into the light of things,
Let Nature be your teacher.

She has a world of ready wealth,
Our minds and hearts to bless—
Spontaneous wisdom breathed by health,
Truth breathed by chearfulness.   20

One impulse from a vernal wood
May teach you more of man;
Of moral evil and of good,
Than all the sages can.

Sweet is the lore which nature brings;
Our meddling intellect
Mis-shapes the beauteous forms of things;
—We murder to dissect.

Enough of science and of art;
Close up these barren leaves;   30
Come forth, and bring with you a heart
That watches and receives.

The Fountain

A conversation

We talked with open heart, and tongue 1
Affectionate and true,
A pair of Friends, though I was young,
And Matthew seventy-two.

We lay beneath a spreading oak,
Beside a mossy seat,
And from the turf a fountain broke,
And gurgled at our feet.

Now, Matthew, let us try to match
This water's pleasant tune 10
With some old Border-song, or catch
That suits a summer's noon.

Or of the Church-clock and the chimes
Sing here beneath the shade,
That half-mad thing of witty rhymes
Which you last April made!

In silence Matthew lay, and eyed
The spring beneath the tree;
And thus the dear old Man replied,
The grey-haired Man of glee. 20

'Down to the vale this water steers,
How merrily it goes!
'Twill murmur on a thousand years,
And flow as now it flows.

And here, on this delightful day,
I cannot chuse but think
How oft, a vigorous Man, I lay
Beside this Fountain's brink.

My eyes are dim with childish tears,
My heart is idly stirred,   30
For the same sound is in my ears,
Which in those days I heard.

Thus fares it still in our decay:
And yet the wiser mind
Mourns less for what age takes away
Than what it leaves behind.

The blackbird in the summer trees,
The lark upon the hill,
Let loose their carols when they please,
Are quiet when they will.   40

With Nature never do *they* wage
A foolish strife; they see
A happy youth, and their old age
Is beautiful and free:

But we are pressed by heavy laws,
And often, glad no more,
We wear a face of joy, because
We have been glad of yore.

If there is one who need bemoan
His kindred laid in earth,   50
The household hearts that were his own,
It is the man of mirth.

My days, my Friend, are almost gone,
My life has been approved,
And many love me, but by none
Am I enough beloved.'

'Now both himself and me he wrongs,
The man who thus complains!
I live and sing my idle songs
Upon these happy plains,   60

And, Matthew, for thy Children dead
I'll be a son to thee!'
At this he grasped his hands, and said,
'Alas! that cannot be.'

We rose up from the fountain-side,
And down the smooth descent
Of the green sheep-track did we glide,
And through the wood we went,

And, ere we came to Leonard's Rock,
He sang those witty rhymes   70
About the crazy old church-clock
And the bewildered chimes.

'Strange fits of passion I have known'

Strange fits of passion I have known,   1
And I will dare to tell,
But in the lover's ear alone,
What once to me befel.

When she I loved, was strong and gay
And like a rose in June,
I to her cottage bent my way,
Beneath the evening moon.

Upon the moon I fixed my eye
All over the wide lea;   10
My horse trudged on, and we drew nigh
Those paths so dear to me.

And now we reached the orchard plot,
And, as we climbed the hill,
Towards the roof of Lucy's cot
The moon descended still.

In one of those sweet dreams I slept,
Kind Nature's gentlest boon!
And, all the while, my eyes I kept
On the descending moon.   20

My horse moved on; hoof after hoof
He raised and never stopped:
When down behind the cottage roof
At once the planet dropped.

What fond and wayward thoughts will slide
Into a Lover's head—
'O mercy!' to myself I cried,
'If Lucy should be dead!'

'There was a Boy'

There was a Boy, ye knew him well, ye Cliffs   1
And Islands of Winander! many a time,
At evening, when the stars had just begun
To move along the edges of the hills,
Rising or setting, would he stand alone,
Beneath the trees, or by the glimmering lake,
And there, with fingers interwoven, both hands
Pressed closely palm to palm and to his mouth
Uplifted, he, as through an instrument,
Blew mimic hootings to the silent owls   10
That they might answer him. And they would shout
Across the wat'ry vale and shout again
Responsive to his call, with quivering peals,
And long halloos, and screams, and echoes loud
Redoubled and redoubled, a wild scene
Of mirth and jocund din. And, when it chanced
That pauses of deep silence mocked his skill,
Then, sometimes, in that silence, while he hung
Listening, a gentle shock of mild surprize
Has carried far into his heart the voice   20
Of mountain torrents, or the visible scene
Would enter unawares into his mind
With all its solemn imagery, its rocks,
Its woods, and that uncertain heaven, received
Into the bossom of the steady lake.

Fair are the woods, and beauteous is the spot,
The vale where he was born: the Church-yard hangs
Upon a slope above the village school,
And there along that bank when I have passed
At evening, I believe, that near his grave
A full half-hour together I have stood,
Mute – for he died when he was ten years old.

Nutting

——————————It seems a day,   1
One of those heavenly days which cannot die,
When forth I sallied from our cottage-door,
And with a wallet o'er my shoulder slung,
A nutting crook in hand, I turned my steps
Towards the distant woods, a Figure quaint,
Tricked out in proud disguise of Beggar's weeds
Put on for the occasion, by advice
And exhortation of my frugal Dame.
Motley accoutrements! of power to smile   10
At thorns, and brakes, and brambles, and, in truth,
More ragged than need was. Among the woods,
And o'er the pathless rocks, I forced my way
Until, at length, I came to one dear nook
Unvisited, where not a broken bough
Drooped with its withered leaves, ungracious sign
Of devastation, but the hazels rose
Tall and erect, with milk-white clusters hung,
A virgin scene!—A little while I stood,
Breathing with such suppression of the heart   20
As joy delights in; and with wise restraint
Voluptuous, fearless of a rival, eyed
The banquet, or beneath the trees I sate
Among the flowers, and with the flowers I played;
A temper known to those, who, after long
And weary expectation, have been blessed
With sudden happiness beyond all hope.—
—Perhaps it was a bower beneath whose leaves
The violets of five seasons re-appear
And fade, unseen by any human eye,   30

Where fairy water-breaks do murmur on
For ever, and I saw the sparkling foam,
And with my cheek on one of those green stones
That, fleeced with moss, beneath the shady trees,
Lay round me scattered like a flock of sheep,
I heard the murmur and the murmuring sound,
In that sweet mood when pleasure loves to pay
Tribute to ease, and, of its joy secure
The heart luxuriates with indifferent things,
Wasting its kindliness on stocks and stones,   40
And on the vacant air. Then up I rose,
And dragged to earth both branch and bough, with crash
And merciless ravage; and the shady nook
Of hazels, and the green and mossy bower,
Deformed and sullied, patiently gave up
Their quiet being: and unless I now
Confound my present feelings with the past,
Even then, when from the bower I turned away,
Exulting, rich beyond the wealth of kings
I felt a sense of pain when I beheld   50
The silent trees and the intruding sky.—

Then, dearest Maiden! move along these shades
In gentleness of heart; with gentle hand
Touch,—for there is a Spirit in the woods.

'The world is too much with us'

The world is too much with us; late and soon,   1
Getting and spending, we lay waste our powers:
Little we see in nature that is ours;
We have given our hearts away, a sordid boon!
This Sea that bares her bosom to the moon;
The Winds that will be howling at all hours
And are up-gathered now like sleeping flowers;
For this, for every thing, we are out of tune;
It moves us not—Great God! I'd rather be
A Pagan suckled in a creed outworn;   10
So might I, standing on this pleasant lea,
Have glimpses that would make me less forlorn;
Have sight of Proteus coming from the sea;
Or hear old Triton blow his wreathed horn.

Composed Upon Westminster Bridge

Sept. 2, 1802

Earth has not any thing to shew more fair: 1
Dull would he be of soul who could pass by
A sight so touching in its majesty:
This City now doth like a garment wear
The beauty of the morning; silent, bare,
Ships, towers, domes, theatres, and temples lie
Open unto the fields, and to the sky;
All bright and glittering in the smokeless air.
Never did sun more beautifully steep
In his first splendor valley, rock, or hill; 10
Ne'er saw I, never felt, a calm so deep!
The river glideth at his own sweet will:
Dear God! the very houses seem asleep;
And all that mighty heart is lying still!

The Solitary Reaper

Behold her, single in the field,   1
Yon solitary Highland Lass!
Reaping and singing by herself;
Stop here, or gently pass!
Alone she cuts, and binds the grain,
And sings a melancholy strain;
O listen! for the Vale profound
Is overflowing with the sound.

No Nightingale did ever chaunt
So sweetly to reposing bands   10
Of Travellers in some shady haunt,
Among Arabian Sands:
No sweeter voice was ever heard
In spring-time from the Cuckoo-bird,
Breaking the silence of the seas
Among the farthest Hebrides.

Will no one tell me what she sings?
Perhaps the plaintive numbers flow
For old, unhappy, far-off things,
And battles long ago: 20
Or is it some more humble lay,
Familiar matter of today?
Some natural sorrow, loss, or pain,
That has been, and may be again!

Whate'er the theme, the Maiden sang
As if her song could have no ending;
I saw her singing at her work,
And o'er the sickle bending;
I listened till I had my fill:
And, as I mounted up the hill,   30
The music in my heart I bore,
Long after it was heard no more.

Elegiac Stanzas

Suggested by a picture of Peele Castle, in a storm,
painted by Sir George Beaumont

I was thy Neighbour once, thou rugged Pile!   1
Four summer weeks I dwelt in sight of thee:
I saw thee every day; and all the while
Thy Form was sleeping on a glassy sea.

So pure the sky, so quiet was the air!
So like, so very like, was day to day!
Whene'er I looked, thy Image still was there;
It trembled, but it never passed away.

How perfect was the calm! it seemed no sleep;
No mood, which season takes away, or brings: 10
I could have fancied that the mighty Deep
Was even the gentlest of all gentle Things.

Ah! THEN, if mine had been the Painter's hand,
To express what then I saw; and add the gleam,
The light that never was, on sea or land,
The consecration, and the Poet's dream;

I would have planted thee, thou hoary Pile!
Amid a world how different from this!
Beside a sea that could not cease to smile;
On tranquil land, beneath a sky of bliss: 20

Thou shouldst have seemed a treasure-house, a mine
Of peaceful years; a chronicle of heaven:—
Of all the sunbeams that did ever shine
The very sweetest had to thee been given.

A Picture had it been of lasting ease,
Elysian quiet, without toil or strife;
No motion but the moving tide, a breeze,
Or merely silent Nature's breathing life.

Such, in the fond delusion of my heart,
Such Picture would I at that time have made: 30
And seen the soul of truth in every part;
A faith, a trust, that could not be betrayed.

So once it would have been,—'tis so no more;
I have submitted to a new controul:
A power is gone, which nothing can restore;
A deep distress hath humanized my Soul.

Not for a moment could I now behold
A smiling sea and be what I have been:
The feeling of my loss will ne'er be old;
This, which I know, I speak with mind serene.   40

Then, Beaumont, Friend! who would have been the Friend,
If he had lived, of Him whom I deplore,
This Work of thine I blame not, but commend;
This sea in anger, and the dismal shore.

Oh 'tis a passionate Work!—yet wise and well;
Well chosen is the spirit that is here;
That Hulk which labours in the deadly swell,
This rueful sky, this pageantry of fear!

And this huge Castle, standing here sublime,
I love to see the look with which it braves,   50
Cased in the unfeeling armour of old time,
The light'ning, the fierce wind, and trampling waves.

Farewell, farewell the Heart that lives alone,
Housed in a dream, at distance from the Kind!
Such happiness, wherever it be known,
Is to be pitied; for 'tis surely blind.

But welcome fortitude, and patient chear,
And frequent sights of what is to be borne!
Such sights, or worse, as are before me here.—
Not without hope we suffer and we mourn.   60

St Paul's

Pressed with conflicting thoughts of love and fear   1
I parted from thee, Friend! and took my way
Through the great City, pacing with an eye
Downcast, ear sleeping, and feet masterless
That were sufficient guide unto themselves,
And step by step went pensively. Now, mark!
Not how my trouble was entirely hushed,
(That might not be) but how by sudden gift,
Gift of Imagination's holy power,
My soul in her uneasiness received   10
An anchor of stability. It chanced
That while I thus was pacing I raised up
My heavy eyes and instantly beheld,
Saw at a glance in that familiar spot,
A visionary scene—a length of street
Laid open in its morning quietness,
Deep, hollow, unobstructed, vacant, smooth,
And white with winter's purest white, as fair,
As fresh and spotless as he ever sheds
On field or mountain. Moving Form was none   20
Save here and there a shadowy Passenger,
Slow, shadowy, silent, dusky, and beyond
And high above this winding length of street,
This noiseless and unpeopled avenue,
Pure, silent, solemn, beautiful, was seen
The huge majestic Temple of St Paul
In awful sequestration, through a veil,
Through its own sacred veil of falling snow

CHRISTINA **ROSSETTI**

A Birthday

My heart is like a singing bird   1
Whose nest is in a watered shoot;
My heart is like an apple tree
Whose boughs are bent with thickset fruit;
My heart is like a rainbow shell
That paddles in a halcyon sea;
My heart is gladder than all these
Because my love is come to me.

Raise me a dais of silk and down;
Hang it with vair and purple dyes;   10
Carve it in doves and pomegranates,
And peacocks with a hundred eyes;
Work it in gold and silver grapes,
In leaves and silver fleurs-de-lys;
Because the birthday of my life
Is come, my love is come to me.

Song

When I am dead, my dearest,   1
Sing no sad songs for me;
Plant thou no roses at my head,
Nor shady cypress tree:
Be the green grass above me
With showers and dewdrops wet;
And if thou wilt, remember,
And if thou wilt, forget.

I shall not see the shadows,
I shall not feel the rain;   10
I shall not hear the nightingale
Sing on, as if in pain:
And dreaming through the twilight
That doth not rise nor set,
Haply I may remember,
And haply may forget.

Up-hill

Does the road wind up-hill all the way?   1
Yes, to the very end.
Will the day's journey take the whole long day?
From morn to night, my friend.

But is there for the night a resting-place?
A roof for when the slow dark hours begin.
May not the darkness hide it from my face?
You cannot miss that inn.

Shall I meet other wayfarers at night?
Those who have gone before.   10
Then must I knock, or call when just in sight?
They will not keep you standing at that door.

Shall I find comfort, travel-sore and weak?
Of labour you shall find the sum.
Will there be beds for me and all who seek?
Yea, beds for all who come.

Remember

Remember me when I am gone away,   1
Gone far away into the silent land;
When you can no more hold me by the hand,
Nor I half turn to go yet turning stay.
Remember me when no more day by day
You tell me of our future that you planned:
Only remember me; you understand
It will be late to counsel then or pray.
Yet if you should forget me for a while
And afterwards remember, do not grieve: 10
For if the darkness and corruption leave
A vestige of the thoughts that once I had,
Better by far you should forget and smile
Than that you should remember and be sad.

Echo

Come to me in the silence of the night;   1
Come in the speaking silence of a dream;
Come with soft rounded cheeks and eyes as bright
As sunlight on a stream;
Come back in tears,
O memory, hope, love of finished years.

Oh dream how sweet, too sweet, too bitter sweet,
Whose wakening should have been in Paradise,
Where souls brimfull of love abide and meet;
Where thirsting longing eyes   10
Watch the slow door
That opening, letting in, lets out no more.

Yet come to me in dreams, that I may live
My very life again tho' cold in death:
Come back to me in dreams, that I may give
Pulse for pulse, breath for breath:
Speak low, lean low,
As long ago, my love, how long ago.

Twice

I took my heart in my hand   1
(O my love, O my love),
I said: Let me fall or stand,
Let me live or die,
But this once hear me speak—
(O my love, O my love)—
Yet a woman's words are weak;
You should speak, not I.

You took my heart in your hand
With a friendly smile,   10
With a critical eye you scanned,
Then set it down,
And said: It is still unripe,
Better wait awhile;
Wait while the skylarks pipe,
Till the corn grows brown.

As you set it down it broke—
Broke, but I did not wince;
I smiled at the speech you spoke,
At your judgment that I heard: 20
But I have not often smiled
Since then, nor questioned since,
Nor cared for corn-flowers wild,
Nor sung with the singing bird.

I take my heart in my hand,
O my God, O my God,
My broken heart in my hand:
Thou hast seen, judge Thou.
My hope was written on sand,
O my God, O my God;   30
Now let Thy judgment stand—
Yea, judge me now.

This contemned of a man,
This marred one heedless day,
This heart take Thou to scan
Both within and without:
Refine with fire its gold,
Purge Thou its dross away—
Yea hold it in Thy hold,
Whence none can pluck it out.   40

I take my heart in my hand—
I shall not die, but live—
Before Thy face I stand;
I, for Thou callest such:
All that I have I bring,
All that I am I give,
Smile Thou and I shall sing,
But shall not question much.

Maude Clare

Out of the church she followed them   1
With a lofty step and mien:
His bride was like a village maid,
Maude Clare was like a queen.

"Son Thomas," his lady mother said,
With smiles, almost with tears:
"May Nell and you but live as true
As we have done for years;

"Your father thirty years ago
Had just your tale to tell;   10
But he was not so pale as you,
Nor I so pale as Nell."

My lord was pale with inward strife,
And Nell was pale with pride;
My lord gazed long on pale Maude Clare
Or ever he kissed the bride.

"Lo, I have brought my gift, my lord,
Have brought my gift," she said:
"To bless the hearth, to bless the board,
To bless the marriage-bed.   20

"Here's my half of the golden chain
You wore about your neck,
That day we waded ankle-deep
For lilies in the beck:

"Here's my half of the faded leaves
We plucked from budding bough,
With feet amongst the lily leaves,—
The lilies are budding now."

He strove to match her scorn with scorn,
He faltered in his place: 30
"Lady," he said,— "Maude Clare," he said,—
"Maude Clare:":— and hid his face.

She turn'd to Nell: "My Lady Nell,
I have a gift for you;
Tho', were it fruit, the bloom were gone,
Or, were it flowers, the dew.

"Take my share of a fickle heart,
Mine of a paltry love:
Take it or leave it as you will,
I wash my hands thereof."   40

"And what you leave," said Nell, "I'll take,
And what you spurn, I'll wear;
For he's my lord for better and worse,
And him I love, Maude Clare.

"Yea, tho' you're taller by the head,
More wise, and much more fair;
I'll love him till he loves me best,
Me best of all, Maude Clare."

Shut Out

The door was shut. I looked between 1
Its iron bars; and saw it lie,
My garden, mine, beneath the sky,
Pied with all flowers bedewed and green:

From bough to bough the song-birds crossed,
From flower to flower the moths and bees;
With all its nests and stately trees
It had been mine, and it was lost.

A shadowless spirit kept the gate,
Blank and unchanging like the grave. 10
I peering thro', said; "Let me have
Some buds to cheer my outcast state."

He answered not. "Or give me, then,
But one small twig from shrub or tree;
And bid my home remember me
Until I come to it again."

The spirit was silent; but he took
Mortar and stone to build a wall;
He left no loophole great or small
Thro' which my straining eyes might look: 20

So now I sit here quite alone
Blinded with tears; nor grieve for that,
For nought is left worth looking at
Since my delightful land is gone.

A violet bed is budding near,
Wherein a lark has made her nest:
And good they are, but not the best;
And dear they are, but not so dear.

A Better Resurrection

I have no wit, no words, no tears;   1
My heart within me like a stone
Is numbed too much for hopes or fears;
Look right, look left, I dwell alone;
I lift mine eyes, but dimmed with grief
No everlasting hills I see;
My life is in the falling leaf:
O Jesus, quicken me.

My life is like a faded leaf,
My harvest dwindled to a husk;   10
Truly my life is void and brief
And tedious in the barren dusk;
My life is like a frozen thing,
No bud nor greenness can I see:
Yet rise it shall—the sap of Spring;
O Jesus, rise in me.

My life is like a broken bowl,
A broken bowl that cannot hold
One drop of water for my soul
Or cordial in the searching cold;   20
Cast in the fire the perished thing,
Melt and remould it, till it be
A royal cup for Him my King:
O Jesus, drink of me.

Winter: My Secret

I tell my secret? No indeed, not I: 1
Perhaps some day, who knows?
But not today; it froze, and blows, and snows,
And you're too curious: fie!
You want to hear it? well:
Only, my secret's mine, and I won't tell.

Or, after all, perhaps there's none:
Suppose there is no secret after all,
But only just my fun.
Today's a nipping day, a biting day;   10
In which one wants a shawl,
A veil, a cloak, and other wraps:
I cannot ope to every one who taps,
And let the draughts come whistling thro' my hall;
Come bounding and surrounding me,
Come buffeting, astounding me,
Nipping and clipping thro' my wraps and all.
I wear my mask for warmth: who ever shows
His nose to Russian snows
To be pecked at by every wind that blows?   20
You would not peck? I thank you for good will,
Believe, but leave that truth untested still.

Spring's an expansive time: yet I don't trust
March with its peck of dust,
Nor April with its rainbow-crowned brief showers,
Nor even May, whose flowers
One frost may wither thro' the sunless hours.

Perhaps some languid summer day,
When drowsy birds sing less and less,
And golden fruit is ripening to excess,   30
If there's not too much sun nor too much cloud,
And the warm wind is neither still nor loud,
Perhaps my secret I may say,
Or you may guess.

Good Friday

Am I a stone and not a sheep   1
That I can stand, O Christ, beneath Thy Cross,
To number drop by drop Thy Blood's slow loss,
And yet not weep?

Not so those women loved
Who with exceeding grief lamented Thee;
Not so fallen Peter weeping bitterly;
Not so the thief was moved;

Not so the Sun and Moon
Which hid their faces in a starless sky,   10
A horror of great darkness at broad noon—
I, only I.

Yet give not o'er,
But seek Thy sheep, true Shepherd of the flock;
Greater than Moses, turn and look once more
And smite a rock.

Despised and Rejected

My sun has set, I dwell   1
In darkness as a dead man out of sight;
And none remains, not one, that I should tell
To him mine evil plight
This bitter night.
I will make fast my door
That hollow friends may trouble me no more.

"Friend, open to Me."— Who is this that calls?
Nay, I am deaf as are my walls:
Cease crying, for I will not hear   10
Thy cry of hope or fear.
Others were dear,
Others forsook me: what art thou indeed
That I should heed
Thy lamentable need?
Hungry should feed,
Or stranger lodge thee here?

"Friend, My Feet bleed.
Open thy door to Me and comfort Me."
I will not open, trouble me no more.   20
Go on thy way footsore,
I will not rise and open unto thee.

"Then is it nothing to thee? Open, see
Who stands to plead with thee.
Open, lest I should pass thee by, and thou
One day entreat My Face
And howl for grace,
And I be deaf as thou art now.
Open to Me."

Then I cried out upon him: Cease,   30
Leave me in peace:
Fear not that I should crave
Aught thou mayst have.
Leave me in peace, yea trouble me no more,
Lest I arise and chase thee from my door.
What, shall I not be let
Alone, that thou dost vex me yet?

But all night long that voice spake urgently:
"Open to Me."
Still harping in mine ears: 40
"Rise, let Me in."
Pleading with tears:
"Open to Me that I may come to thee."
While the dew dropped, while the dark hours were cold
"My Feet bleed, see My Face,
See My Hands bleed that bring thee grace,
My Heart doth bleed for thee,
Open to Me."

So till the break of day:
Then died away   50
That voice, in silence as of sorrow;
Then footsteps echoing like a sigh
Passed me by,
Lingering footsteps slow to pass.
On the morrow
I saw upon the grass
Each footprint marked in blood, and on my door
The mark of blood for evermore.

The Lowest Place

Give me the lowest place: not that I dare   1
Ask for that lowest place, but Thou hast died
That I might live and share
Thy glory by Thy side.

Give me the lowest place: or if for me
That lowest place too high, make one more low
Where I may sit and see
My God and love Thee so.

"Summer is Ended"

To think that this meaningless thing was ever a rose,   1
Scentless, colourless, *this*!
Will it ever be thus (who knows?)
Thus with our bliss,
If we wait till the close?

Tho' we care not to wait for the end, there comes the end
Sooner, later, at last,
Which nothing can mar, nothing mend:
An end locked fast,
Bent we cannot re-bend.   10

To Lalla, reading my verses topsy-turvy

Darling little Cousin,   1
With your thoughtful look
Reading topsy-turvy
From a printed book

English hieroglyphics,
More mysterious
To you, than Egyptian
Ones would be to us;—

Leave off for a minute
Studying, and say   10
What is the impression
That those marks convey?

Only solemn silence,
And a wondering smile:
But your eyes are lifted
Unto mine the while.

In their gaze so steady
I can surely trace
That a happy spirit
Lighteth up your face.   20

Tender, happy spirit,
Innocent and pure;
Teaching more than science,
And than learning more.

How should I give answer
To that asking look?
Darling little Cousin
Go back to your book.

Read on: if you knew it,
You have cause to boast:—   30
You are much the wisest,
Though I know the most.

SECTION THREE

WILFRED **OWEN**

Strange Meeting

It seemed that out of battle I escaped   1
Down some profound dull tunnel, long since scooped
Through granites which titanic wars had groined.

Yet also there encumbered sleepers groaned,
Too fast in thought or death to be bestirred.
Then, as I probed them, one sprang up, and stared
With piteous recognition in fixed eyes,
Lifting distressful hands, as if to bless.
And by his smile, I knew that sullen hall, –
By his dead smile I knew we stood in Hell.   10

With a thousand pains that vision's face was grained;
Yet no blood reached there from the upper ground,
And no guns thumped, or down the flues made moan.
'Strange friend,' I said, 'here is no cause to mourn.'
'None,' said that other, 'save the undone years,
The hopelessness. Whatever hope is yours,
Was my life also; I went hunting wild
After the wildest beauty in the world,
Which lies not calm in eyes, or braided hair,
But mocks the steady running of the hour,   20
And if it grieves, grieves richlier than here.
For by my glee might many men have laughed,
And of my weeping something had been left,
Which must die now. I mean the truth untold,
The pity of war, the pity war distilled.
Now men will go content with what we spoiled,
Or, discontent, boil bloody, and be spilled.
They will be swift with swiftness of the tigress.
None will break ranks, though nations trek from progress.
Courage was mine, and I had mystery,   30
Wisdom was mine, and I had mastery:

To miss the march of this retreating world
Into vain citadels that are not walled.
Then, when much blood had clogged their chariot-wheels,
I would go up and wash them from sweet wells,
Even with truths that lie too deep for taint.
I would have poured my spirit without stint
But not through wounds; not on the cess of war.
Foreheads of men have bled where no wounds were.

'I am the enemy you killed, my friend.   40
I knew you in this dark: for so you frowned
Yesterday through me as you jabbed and killed.
I parried; but my hands were loath and cold.
Let us sleep now...'

Insensibility

I
Happy are men who yet before they are killed   1
Can let their veins run cold.
Whom no compassion fleers
Or makes their feet
Sore on the alleys cobbled with their brothers.
The front line withers.
But they are troops who fade, not flowers,
For poets' tearful fooling:
Men, gaps for filling:
Losses, who might have fought   10
Longer; but no one bothers.

II
And some cease feeling
Even themselves or for themselves.
Dullness best solves
The tease and doubt of shelling,
And Chance's strange arithmetic
Comes simpler than the reckoning of their shilling.
They keep no check on armies' decimation.

III

Happy are these who lose imagination:
They have enough to carry with ammunition.   20
Their spirit drags no pack.
Their old wounds, save with cold, can not more ache.
Having seen all things red,
Their eyes are rid
Of the hurt of the colour of blood for ever.
And terror's first constriction over,
Their hearts remain small-drawn.
Their senses in some scorching cautery of battle
Now long since ironed,
Can laugh among the dying, unconcerned.   30

IV

Happy the soldier home, with not a notion
How somewhere, every dawn, some men attack,
And many sighs are drained.
Happy the lad whose mind was never trained:
His days are worth forgetting more than not.
He sings along the march
Which we march taciturn, because of dusk,
The long, forlorn, relentless trend
From larger day to huger night.

V
We wise, who with a thought besmirch   40
Blood over all our soul,
How should we see our task
But through his blunt and lashless eyes?
Alive, he is not vital overmuch;
Dying, not mortal overmuch;
Nor sad, nor proud,
Nor curious at all.
He cannot tell
Old men's placidity from his.

VI
But cursed are dullards whom no cannon stuns,   50
That they should be as stones.
Wretched are they, and mean
With paucity that never was simplicity.
By choice they made themselves immune
To pity and whatever moans in man
Before the last sea and the hapless stars;
Whatever mourns when many leave these shores;
Whatever shares
The eternal reciprocity of tears.

Apologia pro Poemate Meo

I, too, saw God through mud, –   1
The mud that cracked on cheeks when wretches smiled.
War brought more glory to their eyes than blood,
And gave their laughs more glee than shakes a child.

Merry it was to laugh there –
Where death becomes absurd and life absurder.
For power was on us as we slashed bones bare
Not to feel sickness or remorse of murder.

I, too, have dropped off Fear –
Behind the barrage, dead as my platoon,   10
And sailed my spirit surging, light and clear
Past the entanglement where hopes lay strewn;

And witnessed exultation –
Faces that used to curse me, scowl for scowl,
Shine and lift up with passion of oblation,
Seraphic for an hour; though they were foul.

I have made fellowships –
Untold of happy lovers in old song.
For love is not the binding of fair lips
With the soft silk of eyes that look and long,   20

By Joy, whose ribbon slips, –
But wound with war's hard wire whose stakes are strong;
Bound with the bandage of the arm that drips;
Knit in the webbing of the rifle-thong.

I have perceived much beauty
In the hoarse oaths that kept our courage straight;
Heard music in the silentness of duty;
Found peace where shell-storms spouted reddest spate.

Nevertheless, except you share
With them in hell the sorrowful dark of hell,   30
Whose world is but the trembling of a flare
And heaven but as the highway for a shell,

You shall not hear their mirth:
You shall not come to think them well content
By any jest of mine. These men are worth
Your tears. You are not worth their merriment.

Anthem for Doomed Youth

What passing-bells for these who die as cattle?   1
    – Only the monstrous anger of the guns.
    Only the stuttering rifles' rapid rattle
Can patter out their hasty orisons.
No mockeries now for them; no prayers nor bells;
    Nor any voice of mourning save the choirs, –
The shrill, demented choirs of wailing shells;
    And bugles calling for them from sad shires.

What candles may be held to speed them all?
    Not in the hands of boys but in their eyes   10
Shall shine the holy glimmers of goodbyes.
    The pallor of girls' brows shall be their pall;
Their flowers the tenderness of patient minds,
And each slow dusk a drawing-down of blinds.

Arms and the Boy

Let the boy try along this bayonet-blade   1
How cold steel is, and keen with hunger of blood;
Blue with all malice, like a madman's flash;
And thinly drawn with famishing for flesh.

Lend him to stroke these blind, blunt bullet-leads,
Which long to nuzzle in the hearts of lads,
Or give him cartridges whose fine zinc teeth
Are sharp with sharpness of grief and death.

For his teeth seem for laughing round an apple.
There lurk no claws behind his fingers supple;   10
And God will grow no talons at his heels,
Nor antlers through the thickness of his curls.

Exposure

Our brains ache, in the merciless iced east winds that knive us...   1
Wearied we keep awake because the night is silent...
Low, drooping flares confuse our memory of the salient...
Worried by silence, sentries whisper, curious, nervous,
    But nothing happens.

Watching, we hear the mad gusts tugging on the wire,
Like twitching agonies of men among its brambles.
Northward, incessantly, the flickering gunnery rumbles,
Far off, like a dull rumour of some other war.
    What are we doing here?   10

The poignant misery of dawn begins to grow...
We only know war lasts, rain soaks, and clouds sag stormy.
Dawn massing in the east her melancholy army
Attacks once more in ranks on shivering ranks of grey,
    But nothing happens.

Sudden successive flights of bullets streak the silence.
Less deathly than the air that shudders black with snow,
With sidelong flowing flakes that flock, pause, and renew;
We watch them wandering up and down the wind's nonchalance,
    But nothing happens.   20

Pale flakes with fingering stealth come feeling for our faces –
We cringe in holes, back on forgotten dreams, and stare, snow-dazed,
Deep into grassier ditches. So we drowse, sun-dozed,
Littered with blossoms trickling where the blackbird fusses,
    – Is it that we are dying?

Slowly our ghosts drag home: glimpsing the sunk fires, glozed
With crusted dark-red jewels; crickets jingle there;
For hours the innocent mice rejoice: the house is theirs;
Shutters and doors, all closed: on us the doors are closed, –
    We turn back to our dying.

Since we believe not otherwise can kind fires burn;   30
Nor ever suns smile true on child, or field, or fruit.
For God's invincible spring our love is made afraid;
Therefore, not loath, we lie out here; therefore were born,
    For love of God seems dying.

Tonight, this frost will fasten on this mud and us,
Shrivelling many hands, puckering foreheads crisp.
The burying-party, picks and shovels in shaking grasp,
Pause over half-known faces. All their eyes are ice,
    But nothing happens.   40

The Show

We have fallen in the dreams the ever-living
Breathe on the tarnished mirror of the world,
And then smooth out with ivory hands and sigh.

W.B. Yeats

My soul looked down from a vague height, with Death,   1
As unremembering how I rose or why,
And saw a sad land, weak with sweats of dearth,
Grey, cratered like the moon with hollow woe,
And pitted with great pocks and scabs of plagues.

Across its beard, that horror of harsh wire,
There moved thin caterpillars, slowly uncoiled.
It seemed they pushed themselves to be as plugs
Of ditches, where they writhed and shrivelled, killed.

By them had slimy paths been trailed and scraped   10
Round myriad warts that might be little hills.

From gloom's last dregs these long-strung creatures crept,
And vanished out of dawn down hidden holes.

(And smell came up from those foul openings
As out of mouths, or deep wounds deepening.)

On dithering feet upgathered, more and more,
Brown strings, towards strings of grey, with bristling spines,
All migrants from green fields, intent on mire.

Those that were grey, of more abundant spawns,
Ramped on the rest and ate them and were eaten.   20

I saw their bitten backs curve, loop, and straighten.
I watched those agonies curl, lift, and flatten.

Whereat, in terror what that sight might mean,
I reeled and shivered earthward like a feather.

And Death fell with me, like a deepening moan.
And He, picking a manner of worm, which half had hid
Its bruises in the earth, but crawled no further,
Showed me its feet, the feet of many men,
And the fresh-severed head of it, my head.

Dulce et Decorum Est

Bent double, like old beggars under sacks,   1
Knock-kneed, coughing like hags, we cursed through sludge,
Till on the haunting flares we turned our backs
And towards our distant rest began to trudge.
Men marched asleep. Many had lost their boots
But limped on, blood-shod. All went lame; all blind;
Drunk with fatigue; deaf even to the hoots
Of tired, outstripped Five-Nines that dropped behind.

Gas! GAS! Quick, boys! – An ecstasy of fumbling,
Fitting the clumsy helmets just in time;   10
But someone still was yelling out and stumbling,
And flound'ring like a man in fire or lime...
Dim, through the misty panes and thick green light,
As under a green sea, I saw him drowning.

In all my dreams, before my helpless sight,
He plunges at me, guttering, choking, drowning.

If in some smothering dreams you too could pace
Behind the wagon that we flung him in,
And watch the white eyes writhing in his face,
His hanging face, like a devil's sick of sin;   20
If you could hear, at every jolt, the blood
Come gargling from the froth-corrupted lungs,
Obscene as cancer, bitter as the cud
Of vile, incurable sores on innocent tongues, –
My friend, you would not tell with such high zest
To children ardent for some desperate glory,
The old Lie: Dulce et decorum est
Pro patria mori.

Futility

Move him into the sun –   1
Gently its touch awoke him once,
At home, whispering of fields half-sown.
Always it woke him, even in France,
Until this morning and this snow.
If anything might rouse him now
The kind old sun will know.

Think how it wakes the seeds –
Woke once the clays of a cold star.
Are limbs, so dear achieved, are sides   10
Full-nerved, still warm, too hard to stir?
Was it for this the clay grew tall?
– O what made fatuous sunbeams toil
To break earth's sleep at all?

The Last Laugh

'Oh! Jesus Christ! I'm hit,' he said; and died.   1
Whether he vainly cursed or prayed indeed,
        The Bullets chirped – In vain, vain, vain!
        Machine-guns chuckled – Tut-tut! Tut-tut!
        And the Big Gun guffawed.

Another sighed – 'O Mother, – Mother, – Dad!'
Then smiled at nothing, childlike, being dead.
        And the lofty Shrapnel-cloud
        Leisurely gestured, – Fool!
        And the splinters spat, and tittered.   10

'My Love!' one moaned. Love-languid seemed his mood,
Till slowly lowered, his whole face kissed the mud.
        And the Bayonets' long teeth grinned;
        Rabbles of Shells hooted and groaned;
        And the Gas hissed.

The Sentry

We'd found an old Boche dug-out, and he knew,   1
And gave us hell; for shell on frantic shell
Lit full on top, but never quite burst through.
Rain, guttering down in waterfalls of slime,
Kept slush waist-high and rising hour by hour,
And choked the steps too thick with clay to climb.
What murk of air remained stank old, and sour
With fumes from whizz-bangs, and the smell of men
Who'd lived there years, and left their curse in the den,
If not their corpses...   10
                    There we herded from the blast
Of whizz-bangs; but one found our door at last, –
Buffeting eyes and breath, snuffing the candles,
And thud! flump! thud! down the steep steps came thumping
And sploshing in the flood, deluging muck,
The sentry's body; then his rifle, handles
Of old Boche bombs, and mud in ruck on ruck.
We dredged it up, for dead, until he whined,
'O sir – my eyes – I'm blind, – I'm blind, – I'm blind.'
Coaxing, I held a flame against his lids
And said if he could see the least blurred light   20
He was not blind; in time they'd get all right.
'I can't,' he sobbed. Eyeballs, huge-bulged like squids',
Watch my dreams still, – yet I forgot him there
In posting Next for duty, and sending a scout
To beg a stretcher somewhere, and flound'ring about
To other posts under the shrieking air.

Those other wretches, how they bled and spewed,
And one who would have drowned himself for good, –
I try not to remember these things now.
Let Dread hark back for one word only: how,   30
Half-listening to that sentry's moans and jumps,
And the wild chattering of his shivered teeth,
Renewed most horribly whenever crumps
Pummelled the roof and slogged the air beneath, –
Through the dense din, I say, we heard him shout
'I see your lights!' – But ours had long gone out.

Disabled

He sat in a wheeled chair, waiting for dark,   1
And shivered in his ghastly suit of grey,
Legless, sewn short at elbow. Through the park
Voices of boys rang saddening like a hymn,
Voices of play and pleasure after day,
Till gathering sleep had mothered them from him.

*   *   *

About this time Town used to swing so gay
When glow-lamps budded in the light blue trees,
And girls glanced lovelier as the air grew dim, –
In the old times, before he threw away his knees.   10
Now he will never feel again how slim
Girls' waists are, or how warm their subtle hands.
All of them touch him like some queer disease.

*   *   *

There was an artist silly for his face,
For it was younger than his youth, last year.
Now, he is old; his back will never brace;
He's lost his colour very far from here,
Poured it down shell-holes till the veins ran dry,
And half his lifetime lapsed in the hot race
And leap of purple spurted from his thigh.   20

*   *   *

One time he liked a blood-smear down his leg,
After the matches, carried shoulder-high.
It was after football, when he'd drunk a peg,
He thought he'd better join. – He wonders why.
Someone had said he'd look a god in kilts,
That's why; and maybe, too, to please his Meg,
Aye, that was it, to please the giddy jilts
He asked to join. He didn't have to beg;
Smiling they wrote his lie aged nineteen years.
Germans he scarcely thought of; all their guilt,   30
And Austria's, did not move him. And no fears
Of Fear came yet. He thought of jewelled hilts
For daggers in plaid socks; of smart salutes;
And care of arms; and leave; and pay arrears;
Esprit de corps; and hints for young recruits.
And soon, he was drafted out with drums and cheers.

        *   *   *

Some cheered him home, but not as crowds cheer Goal.
Only a solemn man who brought him fruits
Thanked him; and then enquired about his soul.

        *   *   *

Now, he will spend a few sick years in institutes,   40
And do what things the rules consider wise,
And take whatever pity they may dole.
Tonight he noticed how the women's eyes
Passed from him to the strong men that were whole.
How cold and late it is! Why don't they come
And put him into bed? Why don't they come?

Mental Cases

Who are these? Why sit they here in twilight?   1
Wherefore rock they, purgatorial shadows,
Drooping tongues from jaws that slob their relish,
Baring teeth that leer like skulls' teeth wicked?
Stroke on stroke of pain, – but what slow panic,
Gouged these chasms round their fretted sockets?
Ever from their hair and through their hands' palms
Misery swelters. Surely we have perished
Sleeping, and walk hell; but who these hellish?

– These are men whose minds the Dead have ravished.   10
Memory fingers in their hair of murders,
Multitudinous murders they once witnessed.
Wading sloughs of flesh these helpless wander,
Treading blood from lungs that had loved laughter.
Always they must see these things and hear them,
Batter of guns and shatter of flying muscles,
Carnage incomparable, and human squander
Rucked too thick for these men's extrication.

Therefore still their eyeballs shrink tormented
Back into their brains, because on their sense   20
Sunlight seems a blood-smear; night comes blood-black;
Dawn breaks open like a wound that bleeds afresh.
– Thus their heads wear this hilarious, hideous,
Awful falseness of set-smiling corpses.
– Thus their hands are plucking at each other;
Picking at the rope-knouts of their scourging;
Snatching after us who smote them, brother,
Pawing us who dealt them war and madness.

Miners

There was a whispering in my hearth,   1
 A sigh of the coal,
Grown wistful of a former earth
 It might recall.

I listened for a tale of leaves
 And smothered ferns,
Frond-forests, and the low sly lives
 Before the fauns.

My fire might show steam-phantoms simmer
 From Time's old cauldron,   10
Before the birds made nests in summer,
 Or men had children.

But the coals were murmuring of their mine,
 And moans down there
Of boys that slept wry sleep, and men
 Writhing for air.

And I saw white bones in the cinder-shard,
 Bones without number.
Many the muscled bodies charred,
 And few remember.   20

I thought of all that worked dark pits
 Of war, and died
Digging the rock where Death reputes
 Peace lies indeed.

Comforted years will sit soft-chaired,
    In rooms of amber;
The years will stretch their hands, well-cheered
    By our life's ember;

The centuries will burn rich loads
    With which we groaned,   30
Whose warmth shall lull their dreaming lids,
    While songs are crooned;
But they will not dream of us poor lads,
    Left in the ground.

A Terre

(being the philosophy of many soldiers)

Sit on the bed. I'm blind, and three parts shell.   1
Be careful; can't shake hands now; never shall.
Both arms have mutinied against me, – brutes.
My fingers fidget like ten idle brats.

I tried to peg out soldierly, – no use!
One dies of war like any old disease.
This bandage feels like pennies on my eyes.
I have my medals? – Discs to make eyes close.
My glorious ribbons? – Ripped from my own back
In scarlet shreds. (That's for your poetry book.)   10

A short life and a merry one, my buck!
We used to say we'd hate to live dead – old, –
Yet now... I'd willingly be puffy, bald,
And patriotic. Buffers catch from boys
At least the jokes hurled at them. I suppose
Little I'd ever teach a son, but hitting,
Shooting, war, hunting, all the arts of hurting.
Well, that's what I learnt, – that, and making money.

Your fifty years ahead seem none too many?
Tell me how long I've got? God! For one year   20
To help myself to nothing more than air!
One Spring! Is one too good to spare, too long?
Spring wind would work its own way to my lung,
And grow me legs as quick as lilac-shoots.

My servant's lamed, but listen how he shouts!
When I'm lugged out, he'll still be good for that.
Here in this mummy-case, you know, I've thought
How well I might have swept his floors for ever.
I'd ask no nights off when the bustle's over,
Enjoying so the dirt. Who's prejudiced   30
Against a grimed hand when his own's quite dust,
Less live than specks that in the sun-shafts turn,
Less warm than dust that mixes with arms' tan?
I'd love to be a sweep, now, black as Town,
Yes, or a muckman. Must I be his load?

O Life, Life, let me breathe, – a dug-out rat!
Not worse than ours the lives rats lead –
Nosing along at night down some safe rut,
They find a shell-proof home before they rot.
Dead men may envy living mites in cheese,   40
Or good germs even. Microbes have their joys,
And subdivide, and never come to death.
Certainly flowers have the easiest time on earth.
'I shall be one with nature, herb, and stone,'
Shelley would tell me. Shelley would be stunned:
The dullest Tommy hugs that fancy now.
'Pushing up daisies' is their creed, you know.

To grain, then, go my fat, to buds my sap,
For all the usefulness there is in soap.
D'you think the Boche will ever stew man-soup?   50
Some day, no doubt, if . . .
                                    Friend, be very sure
I shall be better off with plants that share
More peaceably the meadow and the shower.
Soft rains will touch me, – as they could touch once,
And nothing but the sun shall make me ware.
Your guns may crash around me. I'll not hear;
Or, if I wince, I shall not know I wince.
Don't take my soul's poor comfort for your jest.
Soldiers may grow a soul when turned to fronds,
But here the thing's best left at home with friends.   60

My soul's a little grief, grappling your chest,
To climb your throat on sobs; easily chased
On other sighs and wiped by fresher winds.

Carry my crying spirit till it's weaned
To do without what blood remained these wounds.

SECTION
FOUR

ROBERT **FROST**

Mending Wall

Something there is that doesn't love a wall,   1
That sends the frozen-ground-swell under it
And spills the upper boulders in the sun,
And makes gaps even two can pass abreast.
The work of hunters is another thing:
I have come after them and made repair
Where they have left not one stone on a stone,
But they would have the rabbit out of hiding,
To please the yelping dogs. The gaps I mean,
No one has seen them made or heard them made,   10
But at spring mending-time we find them there.
I let my neighbor know beyond the hill;
And on a day we meet to walk the line
And set the wall between us once again.
We keep the wall between us as we go.
To each the boulders that have fallen to each.
And some are loaves and some so nearly balls
We have to use a spell to make them balance:
'Stay where you are until our backs are turned!'
We wear our fingers rough with handling them.   20
Oh, just another kind of outdoor game,
One on a side. It comes to little more:
There where it is we do not need the wall:
He is all pine and I am apple orchard.
My apple trees will never get across
And eat the cones under his pines, I tell him.
He only says, 'Good fences make good neighbors.'
Spring is the mischief in me, and I wonder
If I could put a notion in his head:
'*Why* do they make good neighbors? Isn't it   30
Where there are cows? But here there are no cows.
Before I built a wall I'd ask to know

What I was walling in or walling out,
And to whom I was like to give offense.
Something there is that doesn't love a wall,
That wants it down.' I could say 'Elves' to him,
But it's not elves exactly, and I'd rather
He said it for himself. I see him there,
Bringing a stone grasped firmly by the top
In each hand, like an old-stone savage armed.   40
He moves in darkness as it seems to me,
Not of woods only and the shade of trees.
He will not go behind his father's saying,
And he likes having thought of it so well
He says again, 'Good fences make good neighbors.'

The Black Cottage

We chanced in passing by that afternoon   1
To catch it in a sort of special picture
Among tar-banded ancient cherry trees,
Set well back from the road in rank lodged grass,
The little cottage we were speaking of,
A front with just a door between two windows,
Fresh painted by the shower a velvet black.
We paused, the minister and I, to look.
He made as if to hold it at arm's length
Or put the leaves aside that framed it in.   10
'Pretty,' he said. 'Come in. No one will care.'
The path was a vague parting in the grass
That led us to a weathered windowsill.
We pressed our faces to the pane. 'You see,' he said,
'Everything's as she left it when she died.
Her sons won't sell the house or the things in it.
They say they mean to come and summer here
Where they were boys. They haven't come this year.
They live so far away – one is out West —
It will be hard for them to keep their word.   20
Anyway they won't have the place disturbed.'
A buttoned haircloth lounge spread scrolling arms
Under a crayon portrait on the wall,
Done sadly from an old daguerreotype.
'That was the father as he went to war.
She always, when she talked about the war,
Sooner or later came and leaned, half knelt,
Against the lounge beside it, though I doubt
If such unlifelike lines kept power to stir
Anything in her after all the years.   30
He fell at Gettysburg or Fredericksburg,
I ought to know – it makes a difference which:

Fredericksburg wasn't Gettysburg, of course.
But what I'm getting to is how forsaken
A little cottage this has always seemed;
Since she went, more than ever, but before—
I don't mean altogether by the lives
That had gone out of it, the father first,
Then the two sons, till she was left alone.
(Nothing could draw her after those two sons.   40
She valued the considerate neglect
She had at some cost taught them after years.)
I mean by the world's having passed it by—
As we almost got by this afternoon.
It always seems to me a sort of mark
To measure how far fifty years have brought us.
Why not sit down if you are in no haste?
These doorsteps seldom have a visitor.
The warping boards pull out their own old nails
With none to tread and put them in their place.   50
She had her own idea of things, the old lady.
And she liked talk. She had seen Garrison
And Whittier, and had her story of them.
One wasn't long in learning that she thought,
Whatever else the Civil War was for,
It wasn't just to keep the States together,
Nor just to free the slaves, though it did both.
She wouldn't have believed those ends enough
To have given outright for them all she gave.
Her giving somehow touched the principle   60
That all men are created free and equal.
And to hear her quaint phrases – so removed
From the world's view today of all those things.
That's a hard mystery of Jefferson's.

What did he mean? Of course the easy way
Is to decide it simply isn't true.
It may not be. I heard a fellow say so.
But never mind, the Welshman got it planted
Where it will trouble us a thousand years.
Each age will have to reconsider it.   70
You couldn't tell her what the West was saying,
And what the South, to her serene belief.
She had some art of hearing and yet not
Hearing the latter wisdom of the world.
White was the only race she ever knew.
Black she had scarcely seen, and yellow never.
But how could they be made so very unlike
By the same hand working in the same stuff?
She had supposed the war decided that.
What are you going to do with such a person?   80
Strange how such innocence gets its own way.
I shouldn't be surprised if in this world
It were the force that would at last prevail.
Do you know but for her there was a time
When, to please younger members of the church,
Or rather say non-members in the church,
Whom we all have to think of nowadays,
I would have changed the Creed a very little?
Not that she ever had to ask me not to;
It never got so far as that; but the bare thought   90
Of her old tremulous bonnet in the pew,
And of her half asleep, was too much for me.
Why, I might wake her up and startle her.
It was the words "descended into Hades"
That seemed too pagan to our liberal youth.
You know they suffered from a general onslaught.

And well, if they weren't true why keep right on
Saying them like the heathen? We could drop them.
Only – there was the bonnet in the pew.
Such a phrase couldn't have meant much to her.   100
But suppose she had missed it from the Creed,
As a child misses the unsaid Good-night,
And falls asleep with heartache – how should *I* feel?
I'm just as glad she made me keep hands off
For, dear me, why abandon a belief
Merely because it ceases to be true.
Cling to it long enough, and not a doubt
It will turn true again, for so it goes.
Most of the change we think we see in life
Is due to truths being in and out of favor.   110
As I sit here, and oftentimes, I wish
I could be monarch of a desert land
I could devote and dedicate forever
To the truths we keep coming back and back to.
So desert it would have to be, so walled
By mountain ranges half in summer snow,
No one would covet it or think it worth
The pains of conquering to force change on.
Scattered oases where men dwelt, but mostly
Sand dunes held loosely in tamarisk   120
Blown over and over themselves in idleness.
Sand grains should sugar in the natal dew
The babe born to the desert, the sandstorm
Retard mid-waste my cowering caravans—

'There are bees in this wall.' He struck the clapboards,
Fierce heads looked out; small bodies pivoted.
We rose to go. Sunset blazed on the windows.

After Apple-Picking

My long two-pointed ladder's sticking through a tree   1
Toward heaven still,
And there's a barrel that I didn't fill
Beside it, and there may be two or three
Apples I didn't pick upon some bough.
But I am done with apple-picking now.
Essence of winter sleep is on the night,
The scent of apples: I am drowsing off.
I cannot rub the strangeness from my sight
I got from looking through a pane of glass   10
I skimmed this morning from the drinking trough
And held against the world of hoary grass.
It melted, and I let it fall and break.
But I was well
Upon my way to sleep before it fell,
And I could tell
What form my dreaming was about to take.
Magnified apples appear and disappear,
Stem end and blossom end,
And every fleck of russet showing clear.   20
My instep arch not only keeps the ache,
It keeps the pressure of a ladder-round.
I feel the ladder sway as the boughs bend.
And I keep hearing from the cellar bin
The rumbling sound
Of load on load of apples coming in.
For I have had too much
Of apple-picking: I am overtired

Of the great harvest I myself desired.
There were ten thousand thousand fruit to touch,   30
Cherish in hand, lift down, and not let fall.
For all
That struck the earth,
No matter if not bruised or spiked with stubble,
Went surely to the cider-apple heap
As of no worth.
One can see what will trouble
This sleep of mine, whatever sleep it is.
Were he not gone,
The woodchuck could say whether it's like his   40
Long sleep, as I describe its coming on,
Or just some human sleep.

The Road Not Taken

Two roads diverged in a yellow wood,   1
And sorry I could not travel both
And be one traveler, long I stood
And looked down one as far as I could
To where it bent in the undergrowth;

Then took the other, as just as fair,
And having perhaps the better claim,
Because it was grassy and wanted wear;
Though as for that, the passing there
Had worn them really about the same,   10

And both that morning equally lay
In leaves no step had trodden black.
Oh, I kept the first for another day!
Yet knowing how way leads on to way,
I doubted if I should ever come back.

I shall be telling this with a sigh
Somewhere ages and ages hence:
Two roads diverged in a wood, and I —
I took the one less traveled by,
And that has made all the difference.   20

Birches

When I see birches bend to left and right   1
Across the lines of straighter darker trees,
I like to think some boy's been swinging them.
But swinging doesn't bend them down to stay
As ice storms do. Often you must have seen them
Loaded with ice a sunny winter morning
After a rain. They click upon themselves
As the breeze rises, and turn many-colored
As the stir cracks and crazes their enamel.
Soon the sun's warmth makes them shed crystal shells   10
Shattering and avalanching on the snow crust —
Such heaps of broken glass to sweep away
You'd think the inner dome of heaven had fallen.
They are dragged to the withered bracken by the load,
And they seem not to break; though once they are bowed
So low for long, they never right themselves.
You may see their trunks arching in the woods
Years afterwards, trailing their leaves on the ground
Like girls on hands and knees that throw their hair
Before them over their heads to dry in the sun.   20
But I was going to say when Truth broke in
With all her matter of fact about the ice storm,
I should prefer to have some boy bend them
As he went out and in to fetch the cows —
Some boy too far from town to learn baseball,
Whose only play was what he found himself,
Summer or winter, and could play alone.
One by one he subdued his father's trees
By riding them down over and over again
Until he took the stiffness out of them,   30
And not one but hung limp, not one was left
For him to conquer. He learned all there was

To learn about not launching out too soon
And so not carrying the tree away
Clear to the ground. He always kept his poise
To the top branches, climbing carefully
With the same pains you use to fill a cup
Up to the brim, and even above the brim.
Then he flung outward, feet first, with a swish,
Kicking his way down through the air to the ground.   40
So was I once myself a swinger of birches.
And so I dream of going back to be.
It's when I'm weary of considerations,
And life is too much like a pathless wood
Where your face burns and tickles with the cobwebs
Broken across it, and one eye is weeping
From a twig's having lashed across it open.
I'd like to get away from earth awhile
And then come back to it and begin over.
May no fate willfully misunderstand me   50
And half grant what I wish and snatch me away
Not to return. Earth's the right place for love:
I don't know where it's likely to go better.
I'd like to go by climbing a birch tree,
And climb black branches up a snow-white trunk
Toward heaven, till the tree could bear no more,
But dipped its top and set me down again.
That would be good both going and coming back.
One could do worse than be a swinger of birches.

'Out, Out—'

The buzz saw snarled and rattled in the yard   1
And made dust and dropped stove-length sticks of wood,
Sweet-scented stuff when the breeze drew across it.
And from there those that lifted eyes could count
Five mountain ranges one behind the other
Under the sunset far into Vermont.
And the saw snarled and rattled, snarled and rattled,
As it ran light, or had to bear a load.
And nothing happened: day was all but done.
Call it a day, I wish they might have said   10
To please the boy by giving him the half hour
That a boy counts so much when saved from work.
His sister stood beside them in her apron
To tell them 'Supper.' At the word, the saw,
As if to prove saws knew what supper meant,
Leaped out at the boy's hand, or seemed to leap —
He must have given the hand. However it was,
Neither refused the meeting. But the hand!
The boy's first outcry was a rueful laugh,
As he swung toward them holding up the hand,   20
Half in appeal, but half as if to keep
The life from spilling. Then the boy saw all —
Since he was old enough to know, big boy
Doing a man's work, though a child at heart —
He saw all spoiled. 'Don't let him cut my hand off —
The doctor, when he comes. Don't let him, sister!'
So. But the hand was gone already.
The doctor put him in the dark of ether.
He lay and puffed his lips out with his breath.
And then – the watcher at his pulse took fright.   30
No one believed. They listened at his heart.
Little – less – nothing! – and that ended it.
No more to build on there. And they, since they
Were not the one dead, turned to their affairs.

The Sound of Trees

I wonder about the trees.   1
Why do we wish to bear
Forever the noise of these
More than another noise
So close to our dwelling place?
We suffer them by the day
Till we lose all measure of pace,
And fixity in our joys,
And acquire a listening air.
They are that that talks of going   10
But never gets away;
And that talks no less for knowing,
As it grows wiser and older,
That now it means to stay.
My feet tug at the floor
And my head sways to my shoulder
Sometimes when I watch trees sway,
From the window or the door.
I shall set forth for somewhere,
I shall make the reckless choice   20
Some day when they are in voice
And tossing so as to scare
The white clouds over them on.
I shall have less to say,
But I shall be gone.

To E.T.

I slumbered with your poems on my breast,   1
Spread open as I dropped them half-read through
Like dove wings on a figure on a tomb,
To see if in a dream they brought of you

I might not have the chance I missed in life
Through some delay, and call you to your face
First soldier, and then poet, and then both,
Who died a soldier-poet of your race.

I meant, you meant, that nothing should remain
Unsaid between us, brother, and this remained —   10
And one thing more that was not then to say:
The Victory for what it lost and gained.

You went to meet the shell's embrace of fire
On Vimy Ridge; and when you fell that day
The war seemed over more for you than me,
But now for me than you – the other way.

How over, though, for even me who knew
The foe thrust back unsafe beyond the Rhine,
If I was not to speak of it to you
And see you pleased once more with words of mine?   20

Stopping by Woods on a Snowy Evening

Whose woods these are I think I know.　　　　　　　　　1
His house is in the village, though;
He will not see me stopping here
To watch his woods fill up with snow.

My little horse must think it queer
To stop without a farmhouse near
Between the woods and frozen lake
The darkest evening of the year.

He gives his harness bells a shake
To ask if there is some mistake.　　　　　　　　　10
The only other sound's the sweep
Of easy wind and downy flake.

The woods are lovely, dark, and deep,
But I have promises to keep,
And miles to go before I sleep,
And miles to go before I sleep.

Two Look at Two

Love and forgetting might have carried them   1
A little further up the mountainside
With night so near, but not much further up.
They must have halted soon in any case
With thoughts of the path back, how rough it was
With rock and washout, and unsafe in darkness;
When they were halted by a tumbled wall
With barbed-wire binding. They stood facing this,
Spending what onward impulse they still had
In one last look the way they must not go,   10
On up the failing path, where, if a stone
Or earthslide moved at night, it moved itself;
No footstep moved it. 'This is all,' they sighed,
'Good-night to woods.' But not so; there was more.
A doe from round a spruce stood looking at them
Across the wall, as near the wall as they.
She saw them in their field, they her in hers.
The difficulty of seeing what stood still,
Like some up-ended boulder split in two,
Was in her clouded eyes: they saw no fear there.   20
She seemed to think that, two thus, they were safe.
Then, as if they were something that, though strange,
She could not trouble her mind with too long,
She sighed and passed unscared along the wall.
'This, then, is all. What more is there to ask?'
But no, not yet. A snort to bid them wait.
A buck from round the spruce stood looking at them
Across the wall, as near the wall as they.
This was an antlered buck of lusty nostril,
Not the same doe come back into her place.   30
He viewed them quizzically with jerks of head,
As if to ask, 'Why don't you make some motion?

Or give some sign of life? Because you can't.
I doubt if you're as living as you look.'
Thus till he had them almost feeling dared
To stretch a proffering hand – and a spell-breaking.
Then he too passed unscared along the wall.
Two had seen two, whichever side you spoke from.
'This *must* be all.' It was all. Still they stood,
A great wave from it going over them,   40
As if the earth in one unlooked-for favor
Had made them certain earth returned their love.

Gathering Leaves

Spades take up leaves   1
No better than spoons,
And bags full of leaves
Are light as balloons.

I make a great noise
Of rustling all day
Like rabbit and deer
Running away.

But the mountains I raise
Elude my embrace,   10
Flowing over my arms
And into my face.

I may load and unload
Again and again
Till I fill the whole shed,
And what have I then?

Next to nothing for weight;
And since they grew duller
From contact with earth,
Next to nothing for color.   20

Next to nothing for use.
But a crop is a crop,
And who's to say where
The harvest shall stop?

Desert Places

Snow falling and night falling fast, oh, fast   1
In a field I looked into going past,
And the ground almost covered smooth in snow,
But a few weeds and stubble showing last.

The woods around it have it – it is theirs.
All animals are smothered in their lairs.
I am too absent-spirited to count;
The loneliness includes me unawares.

And lonely as it is, that loneliness
Will be more lonely ere it will be less —   10
A blanker whiteness of benighted snow
With no expression, nothing to express.

They cannot scare me with their empty spaces
Between stars – on stars where no human race is.
I have it in me so much nearer home
To scare myself with my own desert places.

A Leaf Treader

I have been treading on leaves all day until   1
    I am autumn-tired.
God knows all the color and form of leaves
    I have trodden on and mired.
Perhaps I have put forth too much strength
    and been too fierce from fear.
I have safely trodden underfoot the leaves
    of another year.

All summer long they were overhead,
    more lifted up than I.
To come to their final place in earth they
    had to pass me by.
All summer long I thought I heard them
    threatening under their breath.
And when they came it seemed with a will
    to carry me with them to death.

They spoke to the fugitive in my heart
    as if it were leaf to leaf.
They tapped at my eyelids and touched   10
    my lips with an invitation to grief.
But it was no reason I had to go because
    they had to go.
Now up, my knee, to keep on top of
    another year of snow.

Neither Out Far nor In Deep

The people along the sand   1
All turn and look one way.
They turn their back on the land.
They look at the sea all day.

As long as it takes to pass
A ship keeps raising its hull;
The wetter ground like glass
Reflects a standing gull.

The land may vary more;
But wherever the truth may be —   10
The water comes ashore,
And the people look at the sea.

They cannot look out far.
They cannot look in deep.
But when was that ever a bar
To any watch they keep?

There Are Roughly Zones

We sit indoors and talk of the cold outside.   1
And every gust that gathers strength and heaves
Is a threat to the house. But the house has long been tried.
We think of the tree. If it never again has leaves,
We'll know, we say, that this was the night it died.
It is very far north, we admit, to have brought the peach.
What comes over a man, is it soul or mind —
That to no limits and bounds he can stay confined?
You would say his ambition was to extend the reach
Clear to the Arctic of every living kind.   10
Why is his nature forever so hard to teach
That though there is no fixed line between wrong and right,
There are roughly zones whose laws must be obeyed?
There is nothing much we can do for the tree tonight,
But we can't help feeling more than a little betrayed
That the northwest wind should rise to such a height
Just when the cold went down so many below.
The tree has no leaves and may never have them again.
We must wait till some months hence in the spring to know.
But if it is destined never again to grow,   20
It can blame this limitless trait in the hearts of men.